The First Apology Is the Worst

Let's Get It Over With

Jimmy Huston

I wish you didn't need this book.

But you do.

Sorry.

See? That's all there is to it.

Sort of.

Just say you're sorry, and you can throw this book away.

Cosworth Publishing
21545 Yucatan Avenue
Woodland Hills CA 91364
www.cosworthpublishing.com

For information regarding permission,
please send an email to *office@cosworthpublishing.com.*

Dedicated to Clementia
Goddess of Forgiveness

Yeah, you've done or said *something*.

And somebody thought it was pretty bad.

Now you're getting a little heat.

Bad vibes.

And they're not going away.

You may be (or have been) right. This is the worst.

You may be (or have been) wrong. This is the worst.

So you're in some sort of dispute?

That's never a good thing, but some disputes are worse than others.

If your disagreement is with someone who's going to be showing up in your life again, especially if it's someone you're going to need, you're going to have to work something out.

One or both of you is mad.

Things are not getting any better and, in fact, are probably getting worse.

You're sure not going to *apologize*.

Why should you?

That's a good question. Why should you?

This is how some wars start. Granted, this isn't going to grow to a full scale war, but things are not going that well for you now, are they?

Why Apologize?

Because.

You are in a dispute with someone who is important in your life, and who you will continue to have contact with, like it or not.

This trouble is going to color every situation with that person. It is going to get worse over time, not better.

On some level, you need this person. Or you will someday.

The longer you wait to get this straightened out, the worse it's going to get.

You really don't want to apologize but...

Romeo and Juliet

What if the Capulets and the Montagues had worked things out?

Imagine if someone in either family had apologized.

These two legendary lovers would not have killed themselves (and we wouldn't have to watch Shakespeare's play about them).

Alexander Hamilton and Aaron Burr

What if Hamilton had simply apologized to Burr instead of getting shot? They could have *both* danced happily in the finale of the Broadway play. It would've had a completely different ending. As would he.

Julius Caesar

If Caesar had apologized to the Roman senate for crossing the Rubicon, perhaps the "Ides of March" would've had a completely different meaning.

Custer and Sitting Bull

If Lt. Colonel Custer had apologized to Chief Sitting Bull he'd still be alive. Well, maybe not alive, but he would definitely have lived longer than he did. (He just wouldn't be as famous.)

There was probably an awkward moment or two for him at Little Bighorn when he would've gladly traded his fame for a few more years on Earth.

Moby Dick

If Captain Ahab had stopped chasing the White Whale all over the ocean, and apologized for all that trouble, maybe he wouldn't have been sunk like the Titanic. They could've been fishing buddies, like Pinocchio and his whale, or Jonah and his.

Little Red Riding Hood and the Big Bad Wolf

If the Big Bad Wolf had simply apologized to Little Red Riding Hood (and her Grandmother) they could have become friends, and the Woodcutter wouldn't have had to kill him.

King Kong and Godzilla

If the giant ape had apologized to the giant lizard, entire cities in Japan would not have been needlessly destroyed.

And together they could have started the world's largest, most gigantic super-zoo.

They could've been pals.

But noooooooo.

Even the Garden of Eden

Maybe Adam and Eve should have apologized for that whole apple thing. That could have saved the rest of us a lot of trouble over the years.

What about Satan?

Shouldn't he apologize for *EVERYTHING*?

There are lots of different names for the person you're having a problem with.

Enemy. This term is hardly ever used. It's too obvious.

Opponent. Not bad enough.

Adversary. Not insulting enough.

Antagonist. Too pretentious.

Bad guy. Too simple.

Aggrieved. Too fancy.

Dufus. Now we're getting somewhere.

There are a few bad words, too. That's a whole other book.

But who are you usually mad at?

Parents

Moms. Dads. Trouble.

And there's no way out.

There's no one who can set you off more quickly than a parent. Sure, they've sacrificed a lot for you, but still....

If you're a kid, that means your parents are bigger than you, and they control just about everything in your life. Why would you want them mad at you?

Like it or not, you need them for a lot of things. Food. Rides. Money. They really hold all the cards. For now, you'd better get used to apologizing.

In most families there should be lots of apologies flying in both directions at all times.

But, for some reason, there's nothing harder or more unpleasant than the idea of apologizing to *them*. The smart thing is to get it over with. They're going to be your parents for a long, long time, and you're going to need their help all along the way. Just do it.

(Eventually, you'll get a chance to put Mom and Dad in a home. Until then, say you're sorry.)

Siblings

Awww—rats!

Even siblings?

That's taking apologies too far.

Face it. If you've got siblings,
you've got trouble.

Brothers are the worst.

If you have both—

Sisters are the worst.

—*that's* the worst!

Rivals

(It would be impolite to use the term "enemies"—but you get the idea.)

These are the very people that you least want to apologize to.

They already think that they are right and you are wrong—about everything.

You know that it's just exactly the opposite, but—

—an apology will take their mind off you. It certainly isn't going to lower their opinion of you. Maybe they'll stop fixating on you and the things you do. Maybe they'll even leave you alone.

In a way, an apology gives you the moral high ground.

They'll hate that.

Bullies

You should never have to apologize to a bully. Ever.

But you will. Unless you can win the fight.

An apology could be the smart way out of a bad situation.

If a fight was going to solve this, the bully wouldn't be picking on you.

Buddies

Why should you ever have to apologize to your buddies? Because you need them. You really need someone who understands you and will put up with you. Besides, they won't remember it anyway.

With real pals, you should never need to apologize. But you will. Along with the familiarity comes the kinds of intrusions and revelations that can shake friendships to the core.

Don't worry about who's right or who's wrong. Just get it over with.

Then you can get back to playing or hanging out or whatever it is you liked to do together before you got mad.

Peers

Not your pals, but everyone else who is at your level. Classmates, neighborhood kids, cousins, teammates...

One way or another, they're all going to make you mad at some point.

It would take a lot of work to get even with all of them.

It's just so much easier to apologize.

Teachers

You're stuck with each teacher for quite a while, and if you want to move on to the next level in your school career, you have to get along—or at least *seem* to get along.

Teachers aren't easy to fool, but they'll play along. They've got lots of other kids to deal with. They just want it over with—whatever it is.

Principals

If you can't apologize to your teacher, you're gonna get here eventually, so you might as well get ready.

Opponents

The cheers say it all. Beat 'em! Crush 'em! Hit 'em hard!

You're supposed to spend entire games trying to humiliate the other team, then suddenly you have to shake hands. That just feels wrong, especially after all the things they've been yelling at you.

Coaches

You absolutely do not *have* to apologize to coaches—
ever. Unless that coach has the power to make you run
laps. Or do push-ups. Unless that coach decides who
plays which position. Unless that coach decides who
plays and who sits on the bench.

You don't have to love every coach. But, you don't want
your coach to be mad at you. You certainly don't want
your coach to feel like he (or she) has to teach you a
lesson.

Lovers

Maybe you don't need this page. But you will. Might as well start working on it now. With intimacy come all the things that come with intimacy. And they're not all good.

Relationships mean you'll be spending lots more time with someone special, and you can't keep fooling each other forever. One of you is going to slip up.

It doesn't take much. A missed compliment that was expected. A poor choice of anything—from movies to dance moves. Someone was late. Someone took a French fry without asking. Someone didn't call when they should have. Someone smiled (and perhaps flirted) with someone they shouldn't have. Too much of something. Too little of something else. Ugh.

Cops

Whatever happened, get ready to apologize. Cops have all the laws and all the power on their side. Plus they have badges, handcuffs, and a gun. Wherever you think your argument is going, they get the last word.

An apology might get you out of trouble.

You can change your story when you get home.

Or you can get a lawyer. It's cheaper to just apologize.

In-laws

If you don't have them now, they're coming someday. And, you're going to upset them. Maybe it will be on purpose. Maybe not.

Get ready.

Customers

Everyone says, "The customer is always right."

Well, we all know that's not true.

But sometimes with customers we have to pretend.

With customers and clients, apologizing is just another form of sucking up.

Do it.

Bosses

Be smart. Maybe you don't want to have to answer to a boss, but you also don't really want to *not* have a boss—so sometimes you're going to have to apologize.

Pets

They're great. They don't really get mad at you, and even if they did they'd have to forgive you—because you are where their food comes from!

That makes pets the perfect ones to practice apologizing on. They won't know you've "given in."

Damage assessment

Exactly how much trouble are you in?

Maybe an apology wouldn't be such a big deal if it really saved your butt.

Some people proudly state that they *never* apologize.

That usually means one of two things.

1. Either that person is never wrong, and therefore never has anything to apologize for...

...or

2. That person is a jerk.

So, if you *never* apologize—you think you're person Number 1—you may sometimes wonder why you're mad so much of the time.

The answer is—you're really person Number 2.

Naturally you don't think you're a jerk, but what do other people think?

Do you need those other people? Never?

Would you like to not be mad so much of the time?

Tired of Arguing?

Maybe you're wondering, "Why is everybody so angry?"

Well, are you having problems with your mom, and your dad, and your brother, and your sister, and your grandma, and your grandfather, and your teacher, and your coach, and your pals, and your teammates, and your neighbors, and even your pets?

Maybe it's you.

Yeah, if you're having problems with *everybody,* it's probably you.

Maybe it's time to apologize.

It's definitely *you!*

Start apologizing!

Here's the dirty little secret to apologizing.

You don't have to mean it.

You *should* mean it. It's definitely better if you mean it. But you don't have to.

Why would you fake it? Because you need to get on with your life. You need the dumb dispute to be over with.

You get all the same benefits from any apology— whether you mean it or not—except one. Peace of mind.

Both you and the person you've apologized to can move on. You can continue your relationship.

You, however, will still feel a bit off. You can live with it. But, there's a little nagging feeling that things still aren't quite right.

It's your choice. No one else is going to know.

Maybe.

Or, just get over yourself. Apologize.

That's right. You don't have to mean it. It's a strategy, a way to move on with your life without any lingering bad feelings between you.

Yes it's a compromise—a compromise you don't want. But without it, things are worse than the apology itself.

Oddly enough, an apology—as horrible as it seems—doesn't lower the other person's opinion of you. It may surprise them. It may impress them. It may make them think you're a better person than they thought.

Only you will know that it's a lie and that deep inside you lurks the secret dislike of the whole idea. Only you will know that you're still full of bad feelings and that you're not healing at all.

You're just being practical. You're moving on with your life and you need this relationship back where it was before feelings were hurt.

You'll still think you were right, but that may change with time.

Forgiveness

There's a lot of fancy talk about forgiveness, but it's not something you come across very often.

It's different from apologizing. It's not really harder, but it always seems like it is.

Forgiveness is not for the person you're forgiving.

Forgiveness is for you.

It means you're finally letting go of all those bad feelings that have been bothering you. It means you can get on with your life.

And, if you get into trouble again, you'll have a pathway to put that behind you, too.

For forgiveness, you *do* have to mean it.

Start small

Pets. Babies. Maybe a rock? Or a tree. A flower! That's it. Apologize to a flower.

Whisper. Repeat. Louder?

A flower isn't even listening. And it certainly isn't going to tell anyone.

Your secret is safe. You get to work out your apology— without having to actually deliver it. It's good practice.

And flowers smell good, too.

Not like the jerk you're mad at.

Oops. That was a bad choice.

Sorry. (See how it works?)

What if your apology is refused?

Slug 'em.

No, wait. Bad idea. You have the moral high ground—whatever that's worth.

Nod. Then smile. Then walk away the better for it.

You'll know you've won.

And so will they.

How do you apologize?

You're going to hate this—but it's what you need to do.

Say you're sorry.

Say specifically what you did that was wrong or hurtful.

Don't make excuses. Don't blame anyone else.

Maybe say you won't do it again.

After you've done it a few times, it won't seem so horrible. And, you may see that it makes a difference to those around you. In time, you may actually feel better, too.

But for now, you just need to get it over with.

Strangely enough, there are no great apologies in either history or literature or life.

That's because great stories need conflict, and apologies reduce it. Apologies stop things from getting worse.

But, there are lots of apologies that did not get made.

They are called arguments.

Or quarrels.

Or feuds.

Or wars.

The Trojan War. They failed to apologize.

World War I. Nobody apologized.

World War II. Again, no apologies.

Maybe it's time to start apologizing.

So give it a try.

Get it over with.

Just remember.
Apologies are free.
The results are priceless.

I hope this book helps.

If not—

— I'M SORRY!

The End

About the Author

Jimmy Huston is a native of Athens, Georgia, who lives in Woodland Hills, California with his wife and dog.

A sometime screenwriter and film-maker, he sincerely apologizes for all his silly books.

Other odd children's books from Jimmy Huston
www.byjimmyhuston.com

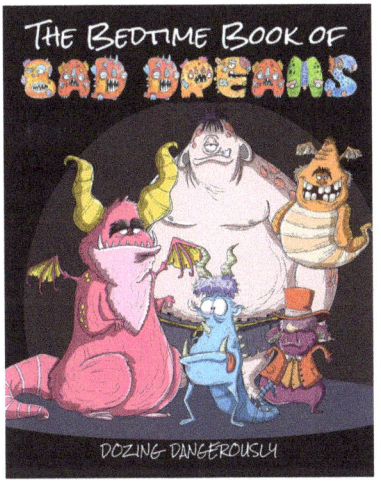

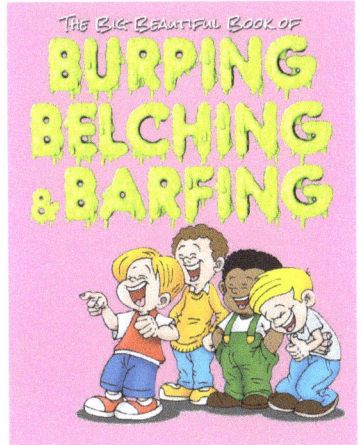
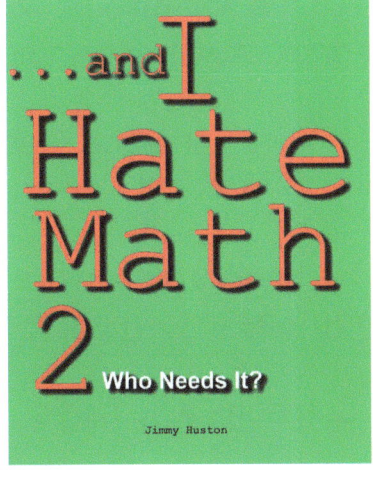

THE DYSLEXIC HANBDOOK

Genius Edition!

LARGE PRINT - BIG PICTURES

Who* buys a book for a kid with dyslexia?

Giving a self-help book to a dyslexic kid is like offering a drink of water to someone who is drowning.

So, have someone read it to you, so you can listen and think about it — and look at the pictures.

This book is also available as an audiobook.
(You'll have to imagine the pictures.)

* Someone who cares.

Other books from Cosworth Publishing
www.cosworthpublishing.com

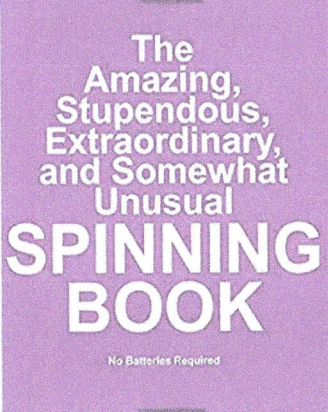

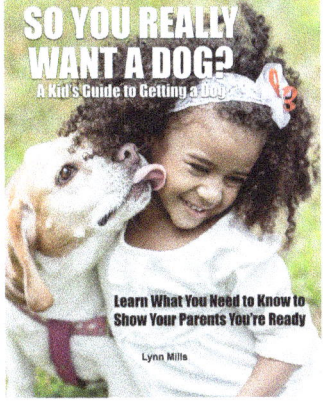

Find it wherever good books are dreaded.

If you're reading this, you will not like this book. It's not for you.

This book is for all the people who are *not* reading this.

They won't like it either, but it's short.

They'll like that.

"I didn't actually read this book. If I had, I would have loved it — but I never will."
Billy

"Hate isn't a strong enough word for me. I loathe reading. I don't even like looking at pictures - which there are none of."
Wally

"This isn't what I wrote about this stupid book."
Zane

"This is an excellent coffee table book, if your coffee table hates to read."
Solomon

"This book made my teacher cry."
David

"My son loved this book. He said it was delicious."
Mr. Jones

"THIS BOOK IS SO DUMB THAT I COULD'VE WRITTEN IT."
Jimmy

www.cosworthpublishing.com

Other books from Cosworth Publishing
www.cosworthpublishing.com

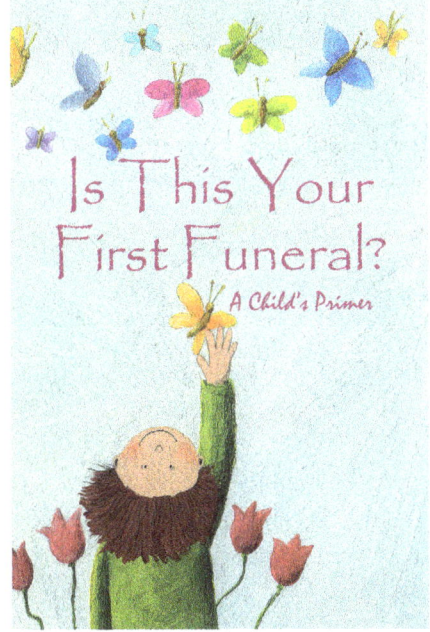

Also Available from Cosworth Publishing

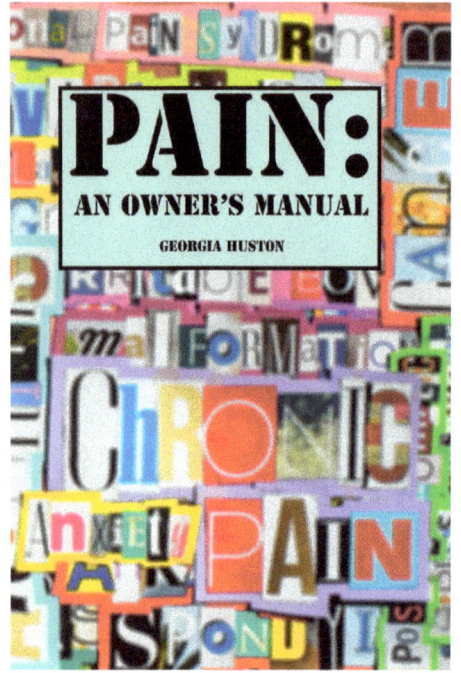

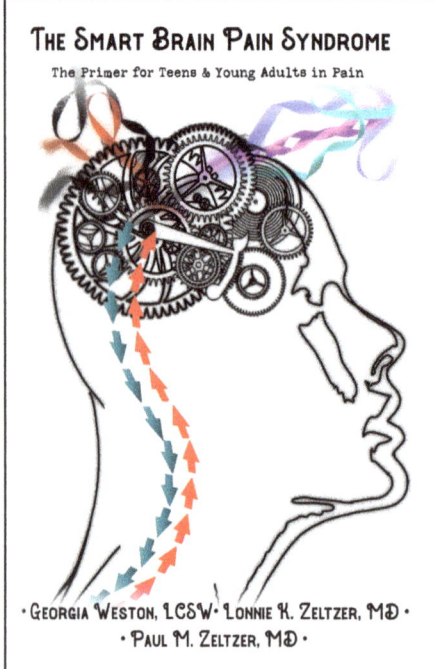

**Thanks for buying, borrowing,
or swiping this book.**

At Cosworth Publishing we truly appreciate that,
and in return, we'd like to offer you one of our
E-books absolutely free—and worth every penny.

Just let us know that you want it, and we'll make
sure that you get it. Send an email to
office@cosworthpublishing.com.

Then, from time to time, we will
let you know via email when
we have a new book that you
might be interested in.

We won't do that very often
because we're basically pretty
lazy, and we don't produce
very many new books.

Reviews are greatly appreciated.

www.ingramcontent.com/pod-product-compliance
Lightning Source LLC
Chambersburg PA
CBHW051243120626
46547CB00014B/1774